ME
WITHOUT
YOU

ME
WITHOUT
YOU

BY LISA SWERLING
& RALPH LAZAR

CHRONICLE BOOKS
SAN FRANCISCO

LIBRARY OF CONGRESS CATALOGING-IN-PUBLICATION
DATA AVAILABLE.

ISBN: 978-1-4521-0298-6

MANUFACTURED IN CANADA

10 9 8

CHRONICLE BOOKS LLC
680 SECOND STREET
SAN FRANCISCO, CALIFORNIA 94107

WWW.CHRONICLEBOOKS.COM

ME
WITHOUT
YOU
IS LIKE...

FOOT
WITHOUT
SHOE

HAIR
WITHOUT
DO

COW
WITHOUT
MOO

DOVE
WITHOUT
COO

KUNG
WITHOUT
FU

BIKER
WITHOUT
TATTOO

GHOST
WITHOUT
BOO

MORNING
WITHOUT
DEW

RESTAURANT
WITHOUT
MENU

ESKIMO
WITHOUT
IGLOO

TANGO
WITHOUT
TWO

PARTY
WITHOUT
YAHOO!

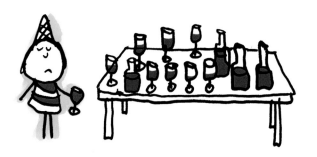

PEAK
WITHOUT
VIEW

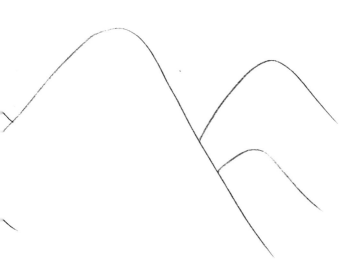

MUCH
WITHOUT
ADO

HARRY
WITHOUT

YOU-KNOW-WHO

BORED
BORED
BORED

PADDLE
WITHOUT
CANOE

CHIMNEY
WITHOUT
FLUE

CLOCK
WITHOUT
CUCKOO

CAT
WITHOUT
MEW

DETECTIVE
WITHOUT A
CLUE

KANGA
WITHOUT
ROO

DOCTOR
WITHOUT

WHO

WRECK
WITHOUT
RESCUE

ZOO
WITHOUT
GNU

HOW
WITHOUT
DO-YOU-DO?

ANTIQUE
WITHOUT
VALUE

RAINBOW
WITHOUT
HUE

TEA
WITHOUT
BREW

PICNIC
WITHOUT
LOO

BELLS
WITHOUT
BLUE

COCK
WITHOUT
A-DOODLE-DO

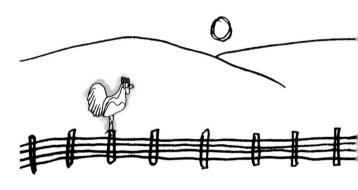

POOL
WITHOUT
CUE

DOCTOR
WITH
FLU

A COOK
WITHOUT HIS
SOUS

A WITCH
WITHOUT HER
BREW

YACHT
WITHOUT
CREW

MOWGLI
WITHOUT
BALOO

SHOO—BEE
WITHOUT
DOO

POLITICIAN
WITHOUT
ISSUE

SAINT
WITHOUT
VIRTUE

MERCENARY
WITHOUT
COUP

SVENGALI
WITHOUT
INGENUE

BALLERINA
WITHOUT
TUTU

RAM
WITHOUT
EWE

COOCHIE
WITHOUT
COO

YABBA
WITHOUT
DABBA—DOOOO!

MUSCLE
WITHOUT
SINEW

SNEEZE
WITHOUT A—

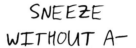

CHOO

DISCIPLE
WITHOUT
GURU

POTTY
WITHOUT
POO

COLD

FONDUE

PANDA
WITHOUT
BAMBOO

RUMBLE
RUMBLE

A PICTURE
THAT'S
ASKEW

A FLAT
KAZOO

A NON-SPICY
VINDALOO

A BOOK
THAT'S
OVERDUE

A KNOT
I CAN'T
UNDO.

BOO

HOO

HOO

HOOOOOOOOOOooo

ME
WITHOUT
YOU!?

WHAT
WOULD I
DO?

BOO!